This book is for you

- you are contemplating, or in the process of, a career change, it planned or enforced.

- you would like to make money out of what you have learned in your career to date.

- you want to understand how to set up a sole practitioner consultancy practice or similar.

- you don't know what you don't know in terms of making the transition successfully.

- you would like to know more about what "good consultancy" looks like.

- you need help in addressing how to sell consultancy services.

- you are keen to achieve "client delight" through your delivery.

- you would welcome someone going on the journey with you.

What people are saying

"Another really useful guide from David Mellor for those looking to grow their businesses. He gives some really practical advice that you can implement straight away. All small business owners should have a copy on their desks!"
Andrew Pullman - People Risk Solutions

"David's a breath of fresh air: he's incisive, direct and perceptive. You'll get no-frills pragmatism with him, as he cuts to the chase, but with the client's interests considered. I couldn't think of a mentor I'd rather have, but David."
Alison Kemp LGSM, MNLP - Director, Switchvision Ltd

"As an organised person, I thought I had factored in everything I needed to get my business off the ground, but there were still things that had not crossed my mind. Both David and his book offer unemotive and practical input into bite-sized morsels that you can digest in your own time. You have to learn to believe in yourself and with expert advice on hand, nothing seems insurmountable!"
Georgina Barber - Director, Aesop Company Solutions

"David's enthusiasm for what he does, coupled with wide ranging thought, good ideas, and willingness to help, make him both a catalyst for change and the ideal mentor."
Mark Lauber, Highgate Capital

"David is a consummate mentor - his depth and breadth of experience coupled with a deep understanding of the theory and practice of business both from a corporate perspective and a small business perspective mean that he has learned what works and doesn't work, written it down in plain English and simplified it while still retaining the value of the many years of experience he brings. I have been in business for 20 years, six as a business coach and mentor myself - what I learned from David in one hour fundamentally shifted my view of my own business. Buy the book, have a chat - nothing to lose, much to gain..."
Gordon Borer, Exceptional Performers

About the Author

Since 2001, David has developed a portfolio of activities which derive principally from 25 years' experience in commercial and investment banking with HSBC and Deutsche Bank. His consultancy activities embrace strategic planning and implementation, and mentoring existing and aspiring entrepreneurs. He is a recognised expert in his field, regularly speaking at conferences and running seminars and workshops. He provides one-on-one and group mentoring to aspiring entrepreneurs, many of whom are aiming to establish themselves as consultants.

He published *From Crew to Captain* in 2010, written for people making the transition from working for big institutions to working for themselves. He has followed that up by launching *From Crew to Captain: A Privateer's Tale* in 2014, which is written for people establishing consultancy practices.

The third book in the trilogy, *From Crew to Captain: Commander of the Fleet*, was released in November 2015 and addresses the "growing pains" issues faced by successful start-ups. He is also co-author of FT Publishing's *Inspirational Gamechangers* which launched in 2015.

He is an Honorary Senior Visiting Fellow in the Faculty of Finance at Cass Business School, where he has run workshops on managing strategic change, entrepreneurship, corporate entrepreneurship, leadership, building high performance teams and sales. In addition, he has acted as course director and provided facilitation and mentoring support to participants in small groups and on a one-to-one basis.

David is a Freeman of the Guild of Entrepreneurs. He holds a Bachelor's and a Master's degree from the University of Cambridge, and is a Certified PRISM Brain Mapping Practitioner.

From Crew to Captain

A LIST OF LISTS

Book 2

by David Mellor

with illustrations by James Mellor

Published by Filament Publishing Ltd
16 Croydon Road, Waddon, Croydon,
Surrey, CR0 4PA, United Kingdom.
Telephone +44(0)20 8688 2598
info@filamentpublishing.com
www.filamentpublishing.com

A List of Lists by David Mellor (Book 2)
ISBN 978-1-912635-76-4
© 2019 David Mellor

Printed by 4edge Ltd.

A quick word from David Mellor...

The purpose of this little book is to help people understand the work they will need to do in order to set up as a sole practitioner or similar. I have made this journey myself, and helped many other people do the same over almost 20 years.

I have selected 10 key areas of establishing a consultancy practice, and given you 10 areas to consider if you are going to move forward with confidence and "eyes wide open".

I hope that the lists will help to inform your reflection, planning and resultant activity.

If the lists create a desire to dive deeper on some of the topics, then I would encourage you do obtain a copy of my second book, *From Crew to Captain: A Privateer's Tale*.

Follow the link to secure your copy!
www.davidmellormentoring.com

If alternatively, or in addition, you would like to meet with me, then please let me know. You can either email me on david@davidmellormentoring.com or call me on 07957 480460.

Speed Dial

The "Speed Dial" Option

A List of Lists - Contents

"You need to go into your new business venture 'eyes wide open', as opposed to 'eyes wide shut'."

Key Challenges

- **Credibility** – how well do you know your sector of choice?
- **Credibility** – how strong is your product knowledge?
- **Credibility** – how much have you done/could you do in terms of publishing, commentating or speaking?
- **Behaviours and Attributes** – have you a desire to achieve and sustain technical excellence?
- **Behaviours and Attributes** – how commercially savvy are you?
- **Behaviours and Attributes** – do you consider yourself to be authentic in terms of what you say and what you do?
- **Lead Generation** - do you have a sales process which you follow?
- **Lead Generation** – how many routes to market do you have?
- **Lead Generation** – do you have the network you need to help you to develop your business?
- **Where does this fit in the consultancy framework?** (see overleaf)

Our survey showed that 50% of people are driven by self-determination and desire to work for themselves, as opposed to being "lost" in a big company

What's been the worst moment?

"Spending a total of over a year working on three separate prospective business partnerships - none of which came to fruition."

Key Challenges	Consultancy Models	Success Factors
• *Credibility* • *Behaviours and Attributes* • *Lead Generation*		

Routes to Market	Sales Process	Tendering
Selling	*Consultancy*	*Services*

Retaining High Value Clients	Personal Branding	Do's and Don'ts
Delivering	*Consultancy*	*Services*

Consultancy Models

- **Subject Matter Expert** – avoid "Jack of all trades".
- **Subject Matter Expert** – industry knowledge, product/service knowledge, or hybrid?
- **Subject Matter Expert** – 100% advisory, 100% operational, or hybrid?
- **Change Agent** – identify action required and create plan.
- **Change Agent** – manage implementation risk and help to manage stakeholders.
- **Change Agent** – transfer knowledge and leave legacy.
- **Trusted Advisor** – are you more valued than purely for your technical expertise?
- **Trusted Advisor** – can you maintain relationships beyond the technical?
- **Trusted Advisor** – have you a well-developed personal brand backed up with strong business acumen ?
- **Where does this fit in the consultancy framework?** (see overleaf)

Our survey showed that the three main requirements in terms of external help were:

1. Finance, including tax

2. IT

3. Networks

What was the hardest part of the practice set-up?

"Creating a USP that was commercial and appealing to prospective clients while remaining true to my beliefs and values. While I could speak passionately about what I believed was right and true it needed to be packaged in a way that clients could easily understand the value that could be gained from it."

Key Challenges	Consultancy Models	Success Factors
• *Credibility* • *Behaviours and Attributes* • *Lead Generation*	• *SME - Subject Matter Expert* • *Change Agent* • *Trusted Advisor*	
Routes to Market	**Sales Process**	**Tendering**
Selling	*Consultancy*	*Services*
Retaining High Value Clients	**Personal Branding**	**Do's and Don'ts**
Delivering	*Consultancy*	*Services*

Success Factors

- **Self-awareness** – understanding yourself better.
- **Self-awareness** – creating your personal brand.
- **Self-awareness** – heightening your awareness of others and adapting your behaviour.
- **Clarity of Purpose** – what business do you want to be in and which values will guide you?
- **Clarity of Purpose** – who is your audience and how will you reach them?
- **Clarity of Purpose** – how will you run your business, what help will you need, and how will you measure performance?
- **Price Integrity** – what pricing options do you have, and how do you get rewarded for the value you are adding?
- **Price Integrity** – do you know your worth?
- **Price Integrity** – be prepared to walk away if the deal is not fair in your eyes.
- **Where does this fit in the consultancy framework?** (see overleaf)

Our survey showed the three

biggest challenges were:

1. Positioning/messaging

2. Sales/securing first client

3. Setting up operational infrastructure

What advice would you give to someone else looking to set up as a sole practitioner?

"Be very focused on establishing your USP - be clear about your story and stick to it. Be aware that the time between establishing a contact and getting paid work can be quite long. Research your market well. Make sure you understood bookkeeping - even if you're not going to do it yourself. Use your existing contacts to kick start your business. Don't panic if you have a slow start! Network, network, network. You have to make yourself known."

Key Challenges	Consultancy Models	Success Factors
• *Credibility* • *Behaviours and Attributes* • *Lead Generation*	• *SME - Subject Matter Expert* • *Change Agent* • *Trusted Advisor*	• *Self-Awareness* • *Clarity of Purpose* • *Price Integrity*
Routes to Market	**Sales Process**	**Tendering**
Selling	*Consultancy*	*Services*
Retaining High Value Clients	**Personal Branding**	**Do's and Don'ts**
Delivering	*Consultancy*	*Services*

Routes To Market

- **Direct** – you identify the targets and prospects.
- **Direct**– you reach out to the targets and prospects.
- **Direct** – you handle the entire sales process.
- **Indirect** – you have reciprocal arrangements with others and find work for each other; no money changes hands.
- **Indirect** – you have reciprocal arrangements with others and find work for each other on a fee-sharing basis.
- **Indirect** – you effectively reward others for finding work for you.
- **Other** – you act as an associate of an established institution.
- **Other** – you team up on business development with like-minded and complimentary businesses.
- **Other** – you run joint events with like-minded and complimentary businesses.
- **Where does this fit in the consultancy framework?** (see overleaf)

Our survey showed
that the biggest
surprise was the length
of time it took to get
some momentum

What was your biggest surprise?

"The length of time from first meeting until it turns into actual work."

Key Challenges	Consultancy Models	Success Factors
• *Credibility* • *Behaviours and Attributes* • *Lead Generation*	• *SME - Subject Matter Expert* • *Change Agent* • *Trusted Advisor*	• *Self-Awareness* • *Clarity of Purpose* • *Price Integrity*
Routes to Market	**Sales Process**	**Tendering**
• *Direct* • *Indirect* • *Other*		
Retaining High Value Clients	**Personal Branding**	**Do's and Don'ts**
Delivering	*Consultancy*	*Services*

Sales Process

- **Qualification** – how do you to turn strangers into cash?
- **Qualification** – does the prospect meet your criteria?
- **Qualification**– do you want the work?
- **Pipeline Management** – how will you track your prospects through the sales process?
- **Pipeline Management** – how will you set conversion ratio targets?
- **Pipeline Management** – how will you deal with sales opportunities that stall?
- **Asking for the Business** – do you know how to differentiate between features and benefits, how to describe your USP (Unique Selling Point), and prove that you can do what you claim?
- **Asking for the Business** – what pricing strategies will you employ?
- **Asking for the Business** – how many closing techniques (i.e. ways of asking for the business) do you have?
- **Where does this fit in the consultancy framework?** (see overleaf)

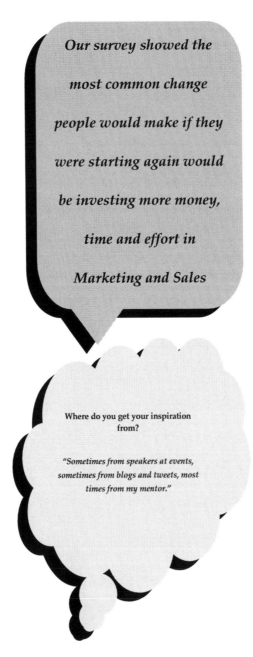

Our survey showed the most common change people would make if they were starting again would be investing more money, time and effort in Marketing and Sales

Where do you get your inspiration from?

"Sometimes from speakers at events, sometimes from blogs and tweets, most times from my mentor."

Key Challenges	Consultancy Models	Success Factors
• *Credibility* • *Behaviours and Attributes* • *Lead Generation*	• *SME - Subject Matter Expert* • *Change Agent* • *Trusted Advisor*	• *Self-Awareness* • *Clarity of Purpose* • *Price Integrity*
Routes to Market	**Sales Process**	**Tendering**
• *Direct* • *Indirect* • *Other*	• *Qualification* • *Pipeline Management* • *Asking for the Business*	
Retaining High Value Clients	**Personal Branding**	**Do's and Don'ts**
Delivering	*Consultancy*	*Services*

Tendering

- **"Path to Assent"** – can you secure a meeting?
- **"Path to Assent"** – can you establish a relationship?
- **"Path to Assent"** – can you reach a conceptual agreement on outcomes?
- **Writing a Bid** – have you done enough research?
- **Writing a Bid** – can you put yourself in the prospect's shoes?
- **Writing a Bid** – have you identified all the stakeholders?
- **Presenting a Bid** – have you prepared thoroughly? (never "wing it"!)
- **Presenting a Bid** – are using a structure that will lead to a positive decision?
- **Presenting a Bid** – are you ensuring that you keep it brief?
- **Where does this fit in the consultancy framework?** (see overleaf)

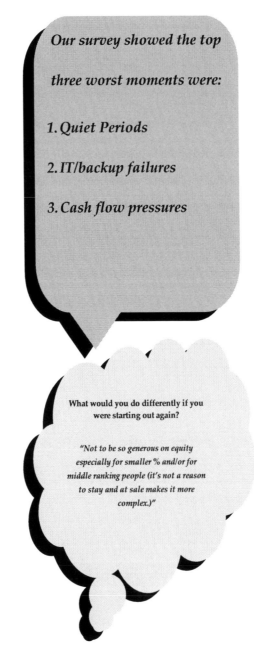

Our survey showed the top three worst moments were:

1. Quiet Periods

2. IT/backup failures

3. Cash flow pressures

What would you do differently if you were starting out again?

"Not to be so generous on equity especially for smaller % and/or for middle ranking people (it's not a reason to stay and at sale makes it more complex.)"

Key Challenges	Consultancy Models	Success Factors
• *Credibility* • *Behaviours and Attributes* • *Lead Generation*	• *SME - Subject Matter Expert* • *Change Agent* • *Trusted Advisor*	• *Self-Awareness* • *Clarity of Purpose* • *Price Integrity*
Routes to Market	**Sales Process**	**Tendering**
• *Direct* • *Indirect* • *Other*	• *Qualification* • *Pipeline Management* • *Asking for the Business*	• *Path to Assent* • *Writing a Bid* • *Presenting a Bid*
Retaining High Value Clients	**Personal Branding**	**Do's and Don'ts**
Delivering	*Consultancy*	*Services*

Retaining High-Value Clients

- **Delivery Process** – do not deviate from the core assignment.
- **Delivery Process** – manage client expectations all the way.
- **Delivery Process** – use checkpoint reviews to ensure all on track.
- **Trusted Relationships** – employ "adaptive behaviour" in all your client dealings.
- **Trusted Relationships** – ensure you deliver on time, to specification, and within agreed budget.
- **Trusted Relationships** – keep in touch with client in between assignments.
- **Bag of Tools** – acquire tools externally or develop your own.
- **Bag of Tools** – stick to tools which you are comfortable with.
- **Bag of Tools** – keep your toolkit under continuous review.
- **Where does this fit in the consultancy framework?** (see overleaf)

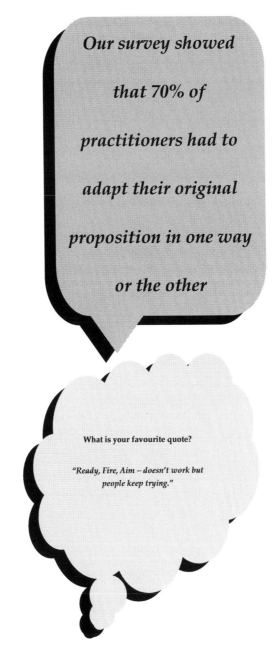

Our survey showed that 70% of practitioners had to adapt their original proposition in one way or the other

What is your favourite quote?

"Ready, Fire, Aim – doesn't work but people keep trying."

Key Challenges	Consultancy Models	Success Factors
• *Credibility* • *Behaviours and Attributes* • *Lead Generation*	• *SME - Subject Matter Expert* • *Change Agent* • *Trusted Advisor*	• *Self-Awareness* • *Clarity of Purpose* • *Price Integrity*
Routes to Market	**Sales Process**	**Tendering**
• *Direct* • *Indirect* • *Other*	• *Qualification* • *Pipeline Management* • *Asking for the Business*	• *Path to Assent* • *Writing a Bid* • *Presenting a Bid*
Retaining High Value Clients	**Personal Branding**	**Do's and Don'ts**
• *Delivery Process* • *Trusted Relationship* • *Appropriate Bag of Tools*		

Personal Branding

- **Attributes** - Ability to be liked.
- **Attributes** – Ability to listen.
- **Attributes** – Ability to enter the client's world.
- **Coherence of Image** – One face to the market.
- **Coherence of Image** – Self-awareness.
- **Coherence of Image** - Authenticity.
- **Networking** – It's not about selling.
- **Networking** – It's about relationship building.
- **Networking** - It's the "glue" in your marketing mix.
- **Where does this fit in the consultancy framework?** (see overleaf)

Our survey showed that over 50% of those interviewed felt that the greatest sense of fulfilment came from winning a new client

What's given you your biggest "buzz"?

"Winning the very first piece of business. That memory will stay with me forever."

Key Challenges	Consultancy Models	Success Factors
• *Credibility* • *Behaviours and Attributes* • *Lead Generation*	• *SME - Subject Matter Expert* • *Change Agent* • *Trusted Advisor*	• *Self-Awareness* • *Clarity of Purpose* • *Price Integrity*
Routes to Market	**Sales Process**	**Tendering**
• *Direct* • *Indirect* • *Other*	• *Qualification* • *Pipeline Management* • *Asking for the Business*	• *Path to Assent* • *Writing a Bid* • *Presenting a Bid*
Retaining High Value Clients	**Personal Branding**	**Do's and Don'ts**
• *Delivery Process* • *Trusted Relationship* • *Appropriate Bag of Tools*	• *Attributes* • *Coherence of Image* • *Networking*	

Do's and Don'ts

- **Top Habits** – Maintain standards.
- **Top Habits** – Focus on delivery.
- **Top Habits** – Capitalise on Emotional Intelligence.
- **Top Disasters** – Promising then failing to deliver.
- **Top Disasters** – Wasting the client's time
- **Top Disasters** - Solving the wrong problem.
- **Top Time Tips** – Use lists (!) to gain momentum.
- **Top Time Tips** – Don't procrastinate over non-essential decisions.
- **Top Time Tips** - Be selfish with your time.
- **Where does this fit in the consultancy framework?** (see overleaf)

Our survey showed

that the biggest

learning point was

picking up "best

practice" from others

What was the best piece of advice you were given?

"I was given lots of advice - but I'm not sure how good it was - or perhaps how well I was listening?! I did get advice on cash-flow - and I can now say that getting payment is really hard - so I would echo the advice on cash flow - get your money in as fast as you can, and push hard on that front - it's critical!"

Key Challenges	Consultancy Models	Success Factors
• *Credibility* • *Behaviours and Attributes* • *Lead Generation*	• *SME - Subject Matter Expert* • *Change Agent* • *Trusted Advisor*	• *Self-Awareness* • *Clarity of Purpose* • *Price Integrity*
Routes to Market	**Sales Process**	**Tendering**
• *Direct* • *Indirect* • *Other*	• *Qualification* • *Pipeline Management* • *Asking for the Business*	• *Path to Assent* • *Writing a Bid* • *Presenting a Bid*
Retaining High Value Clients	**Personal Branding**	**Do's and Don'ts**
• *Delivery Process* • *Trusted Relationship* • *Appropriate Bag of Tools*	• *Attributes* • *Coherence of Image* • *Networking*	• *10 Habits of Top Consultants* • *10 Disastrous Strategies* • *10 Time Management Tips*

Consultancy Health Check - Self-Diagnostic

Score yourself out of 10 on each of the 10 issues (0 being not very good, and 10 being outstanding)

ISSUE

1. I have a strategic plan for where I want to take my business in the medium-term
2. I have a business plan for the current year to use as my operational map and route, with associated goals and objectives
3. I will be working to a robust financial plan based on researched assumptions
4. I will be working to a sales process which helps me to win the business I want and avoid potential timewasters and bad debts
5. I will be working to a delivery process which helps me to create satisfied clients who buy more and/or refer others
6. I have worked out the optimum marketing mix for my business, including routes to market and social media strategy
7. I have established the network I need to enable my business to flourish
8. I know what makes me distinctive and can articulate it
9. I have worked out my personal branding
10. I have quality and comprehensive support around me

If your score is <30 *You should probably talk your idea through with someone and decide what you should do next*
If your score is <60 *You are probably not ready to launch yet - more preparatory work to do*
If your score is >60 *You can press on with some confidence, but keep looking for improvements*

Our survey showed the top three tips are:

1. *Network, Network, Network*

2. *Prepare for things to take longer than expected*

3. *Be absolutely clear about positioning*

What external help/support did you need (or do you wish you had taken)?

"Networks - people who were prepared to put me in touch with their contacts were invaluable".

FROM CREW TO CAPTAIN (Book 1)
Making the transition from working for a big institution
to working for yourself
By David Mellor
with original illustrations by James Mellor

The purpose of this book is to help people understand the transition from working for a big institution to working for themselves. I have made this journey, and helped many others do the same. I want to put the odds in your favour, if you decide to follow suit, that your business venture brings you everything you wish, and that you prosper rather than merely survive. You will find inside a number of practical tips and hints, all garnered from the "University of Life".

I will draw on a broad range of interview material from people who have made or are making this journey, and for whom success has looked very different. It will also draw on a wealth of anecdotal evidence, from my own experience and that of others.

Our journey will take us through three important phases:

1. Reflecting - what does it take to make this transition - and is it for you?

2. Planning - how do you go about preparing to launch your business?

3. Doing - what attributes are going to be really important in the early days post launch?

This book is for you if...

- you have always wondered about what running your own business would be like.

- you are prepared to admit you don't know what you don't know.

- you wonder whether you have personally "got what it takes".

- you think you have an idea but you don't know whether it is commercially viable.

- you are unsure what business skills you will need.

- you don't know what a business plan needs to look like.

- you don't know where to start in terms of raising money.

- you have heard of marketing but are not entirely sure what it is and why you would need it.

- you find the idea of selling scary or daunting.

- you want to put the odds in your favour so that if you do decide to start a business, it will be successful.

FROM CREW TO CAPTAIN: A PRIVATEER'S TALE (Book 2)
by David Mellor
with original illustrations by James Mellor

The user-friendly guide to launching and growing a successful consultancy business

When you're launching your own business, there's nothing like friendly, straightforward advice to set you on the right course. My book *From Crew To Captain: A Privateer's Tale* takes sound business advice and delivers it in a jargon-free, conversational style, making it that rarest of beasts: a business book that is both informative and enjoyable to read!

As a consultant and mentor, since 2001 I have helped scores of people successfully launch their own business. My first book, *From Crew To Captain*, guided aspiring entrepreneurs through the transition from being part of a big institution to working for themselves.

From Crew To Captain: A Privateer's Tale is designed to help people take the next steps of their journey as they launch and, with any luck, grow their new practice. This easy-to-absorb advice and tips are interspersed with useful checklists and light-hearted illustrations as well as one or two cautionary anecdotes!

Drawing from my own successful career as a consultant and through interviews with colleagues, peers and mentees, *From Crew To Captain: A Privateer's Tale* delivers honest, pragmatic advice and offers a simple but highly effective framework that will help consultants from almost any sector maximise their chances of developing a profitable, successful business.

FROM CREW TO CAPTAIN: COMMANDER OF THE FLEET (Book 3)
by David Mellor
with original illustrations by James Mellor

This book completes a trilogy. Book 1 (*From Crew to Captain*) addressed how to make the transition from working for a big institution to working for yourself. Book 2 (*A Privateer's Tale*) looked specifically at how to set up as a sole practitioner consultant or similar.

The purpose of this book is to help people who have set up their own business, proved to themselves and the market that their model works, and are looking to take it to the next level. I have made this journey, and helped many others do the same.

As with the first two books, you will find inside a number of practical tips and hints, all garnered from the "University of Life".

We will look at 4 important aspects of early business growth:

1. Assessing the Situation - what does the business look like today, and why do you want to change it?

2. Achieving Transformation - how do you go about creating and implementing a change strategy?

3. Assessing the Outcome – how do you evaluate success?

4. Building a Consultancy Practice – how do you move from a sole practitioner to a multi-consultant practice?

You may be wondering why I decided to put pen to paper again having written the first two books. One of the issues, which is important to me, is closure. I don't like loose ends, and I had a sense that the first two books left some "unfinished business". I knew I wouldn't rest easy until I had dealt with it by writing Book 3.

So, this book picks up the journey from where the first two books left off. My personal sub-title for the book is "Growing pains and how to deal with them", because that is exactly what the book addresses. Whatever type of business you are trying to build, I hope you will find some "gold nuggets" there.

This book is for you if...

- you have an existing business.

- you have proved to yourself and the market that your business model works.

- you want to understand how to take the business to the next level.

- you don't know what you don't know in terms of making the transition successfully.

- you would like to know more about how to create a value business capable of sustainable profitable growth.

- as a specific issue, you need help in addressing how you move from a sole practitioner model to running a multi-consultant practice.

- you would welcome someone going on the journey with you.